Letts USE ICT YEAR 5

JILL JESSON

CONTENTS

Back to basics	2
Text and graphics	4
Adding more pages	6
Linking pages	8
Graphical modelling	10
Changing shapes	12
Making charts	14
Exploring alternatives	16
Designer school	18
Data search	20
Search AND search	22
OR searches	24
Complex searches	26
Problems with data	28
Checking data	30
Starting spreadsheets	32
Maths machines	34
Spreadsheet sums	36
Budgeting	38
Sequences	40
Control box	42
Monitoring changes	44
Explaining data	46
Glossary	48

Revising the basics 1

Back to basics

Fonts can be altered to suit the context

Pupils should be encouraged to change font after the text has been inserted. Otherwise they may spend a disproportionate amount of time with font choice rather than content.

Skills To Learn | Altering fonts

1. Type:

   > New term 200.....
   > My name is ....
   > This year I am in class ....
   > I am looking forward to......... .
   > Last year I got better at.............. and this year my target is to ....

   Fill in the gaps with your own ideas.

2. Select all the text.

3. To change the style of the text click ▼ in the font box `Arial`, and select a different font.

4. To change the size of the text click ▼ in the text size box `12`, and select **18**.

5. Select the title.

6. In the text size box `12`, click ▼ and select **24**.

7. Click `U` to underline it.

8. Select your name and click `B` to make it stand out.

9. Click after each sentence and tap `↵Enter` to put each one on a new line.

10. Select this year's target and click `I` to make it italic.

Use the align icons to set the text out in an interesting way.

11. Click `cat/katx` to check your work.

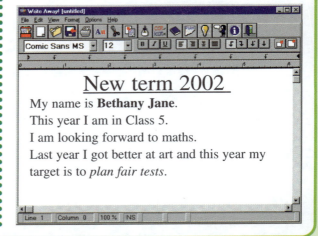

Revising the basics 1

Lesson Link — English

Identify parts of speech.

1 Write a piece of text about a topic you are studying in school.

You could copy a poem instead.

2 Select the prefixes in your text and click **U** to underline them.

3 Select the suffixes in your text and click **I** to make them italic.

4 Select the pronouns in your text and click **B** to make them bold.

Lesson Link — Technology

Design a poster for a new biscuit or bread you have invented.

1 Choose a fancy font for the name of your product.

`Space Biscuits`

Use the same font every time you write the name of your product.

2 Choose a plainer font for the main text.

3 Use the align icons to space out the work in an interesting way.

4 Alter the text size to make the most important parts stand out.

5 Are there any details you need to put in a very small font?

The small print on my tinned food says there are chopped mice in it!

Off Screen

- Try doing each of the above tasks by hand.
- Write about whether they are better done by hand or on the computer.

Explain the advantages and disadvantages of each method.

Revising the basics 2

Text and graphics

PawPrints

Text and graphics can be combined and altered

If shapes are added as frames after the text is written they can be put behind the text by clicking **send to back** from the tools menu.

Skills To Learn | Setting out text and graphics

1 To draw a star click 🔘 and select ⭐.
2 To change the colour set the Fill Colour and Line Colour to yellow.
3 Type: The sun is a star.
4 Click the text to see the handles.
5 Drag the text onto the star.
6 Type: Star facts by Max.
7 Click 𝐭.

Click here to add a frame to the text.

Change the frame style here.

Click here to colour the text box.

Add more information.

1 Start a new text box and type some facts about the stars and planets, tapping ←Enter to put each fact on a new line.
2 Select the text and click 𝐭.

Click here to add bullets or numbers.

Click here to space the text out.

3 Click 📷 to see the picture gallery.
4 Click Geography , select Space and choose a sun picture.
5 Click View and click Zoom out until you can see the whole page.
6 Drag the text and pictures to fill the page.

Revising the basics 2

Lesson Link — Maths

Make a shape chart.

1. Put a circle, a triangle and a rectangle at the top of the screen.
2. Set the `Fill Colour` for each shape to white.
3. Type the name of each shape.
4. Select each title and click `t`.
5. Click `B` and `U` to make each title bold and underlined.
6. Drag the correct title to each shape.

Add as many maths facts as you can for each shape.

Lesson Link — History

See how times change.

1. Ask an adult about the differences between their childhood and yours.
2. Click 📷, select 💬 and draw two white speech bubbles on the screen.
3. Click outside the speech bubble and type your question.
4. Select your question, click `t` and select **Times New Roman**.
5. Click `i` to make it italic.
6. Write the answer and put it into a different font.
7. Drag the two speech bubbles to frame your text.

In what ways were your meals different from ours?

We didn't have so many ready-made meals. My mum cooked lots of stews and we only had tinned foods as a treat.

Off Screen

- Cut a headline and a picture from a newspaper.
- Write a piece of text about the picture explaining the news.
- On another piece of paper list five news events for your school.
- Cut and arrange each item on a larger sheet of coloured paper.

Advanced word processing

Adding more pages

PawPrints

A document can have many pages

Pupils should be encouraged to plan the number and layout of their pages before starting work on a computer.

Skills To Learn — Adding pages to a document

1. On paper, plan how many pages you need for your text.
2. Healthy Living might need three pages, e.g.
   - What is good health?
   - Eating well
   - Keeping fit
3. Open PawPrints.
4. Click `Edit`, select `Add a page` and add two pages.

You will see them appear here.

Click and click `Add a Page`. This is another way to add pages to your document.

5. Click on the page numbered **1**, and type the title: **Healthy Living**.
6. Write an introduction to healthy living on this page.
7. Click on page **2**, type the title: **Eating Well**, and write a short article on healthy eating.
8. Click on page **3**, type the title: **Keeping Fit**, and write a short article on exercise.
9. Click and add food and sport pictures from the `Science` and `General` folders.

Advanced word processing

Lesson Link — English

Plan a story for a young child, e.g. The fable of a lion and a mouse.

1 Plan a page for each part of the story, e.g.
   - Introduction (what is a fable?)
   - Lion catches mouse
   - Lion lets mouse go
   - Lion gets caught in hunter's net
   - Mouse chews net and frees lion
   - Moral (conclusion)... small friends can be a big help.

2 To see the whole page click `View` and select `Zoom out`.

3 Click `t` and choose a large font. Write different parts of the story on separate pages, leaving room for pictures.

4 Click `📷`.

5 Click `Science`, select `Animals` and add pictures to the story.

6 To vary the arrangement of text and pictures click `⊜`, `⊜` or `⊜`.

Lesson Link — Music

Make a musical instruments book.

1 On paper, plan which instruments you are going to write about.

2 To add extra pages click `🗐` and click `Add a Page`.

3 Click `📷` and click `General`.

4 Click `Instruments` and add a picture of a different instrument on each page.

5 Add text about the materials used to make it, its origin, size and type of music it plays.

6 Click `🖨`, and print your pages.

> Put them on cards to make a zigzag book for a display, or keep them as reference cards.

Off Screen

- Plan and make a miniature zigzag book about musical instruments.
- Cut out pictures of instruments from magazines.

7

Introducing multimedia

Linking pages

PawPrints

Pages can be linked

Pupils will need to be reminded that to make a link work they must **right** click it instead of **left** clicking.

Skills To Learn | Linking pages

Add two pages.

1 Click [icon].
2 Click `Add a Page` twice.

You will now have three pages in your document.

3 Type the heading Introduction on page 1, Multiples on page 2, and Square Numbers on page 3.
4 Click on page 1 and type: Right click on a word to know more.
5 Type the words: Multiples and Square Numbers in separate text boxes.

Add a link.

1 Select the word Multiples.
2 Click [icon] and select [icon].
3 Click `Go to a different page of this document`.
4 Click `OK`.
5 Type 2 in the `go to page number` box.
6 Click `OK`.

Now when you RIGHT click on the word **Multiples** you will jump to the multiples page.

Add another link.

1 Click on page 2 and type: Go back.
2 Select the words: Go back.
3 Click [icon] and select [icon].
4 Click `Go to a different page of this document`.
5 Click `OK`.
6 Type 1 in the `go to page number` box.
7 Click `OK`.

Add more information and links.

1 Do the same with the Square Numbers text on page 3.
2 Add text to each page about multiples and square numbers.
3 Add the word Factors to the Introduction page and link it to a new page.

Introducing multimedia

Lesson Link — Science

Solids, Liquids and Gases

1. Plan a set of pages on solids, liquids and gases.
2. Click [icon] and add three pages.
3. Click on page 1, and add the title: Solids, Liquids and Gases.
4. Click [icon] and select `Science`.
5. Add pictures of water and metal.
6. Draw a dotted circle to show gas.
7. Type: Gases are usually invisible inside the dotted circle.
8. Click on the picture of metal and link it to the Solids page.
9. Use one page to explain about the properties of each state.

Add **Go back** or **Go on** buttons to each page.

Lesson Link — Geography

Electronic local information booklet

1. Plan an electronic information booklet about your area.
2. Make a page for each facility, e.g.
   - restaurants
   - sports facilities
   - theatres and cinemas
   - good walks
   - shopping facilities
3. Click [icon] and click and add the extra pages you need.
4. Add the information to each page.
5. Link each page to the Introduction page with a text link.
6. Click [icon] and select `Geography`.
7. Add pictures to each page.
8. Link each page to the next page with a picture link.

Off Screen

- Plan a multimedia presentation on a subject which interests you.
- Make a storyboard diagram to show how the pages are linked.

Use text and picture links on each page.

Unit 5A Graphical modelling

Graphical modelling

Fresco

Images can be created by combining and manipulating objects

Although images can be copied from Fresco to PawPrints, it is not possible to do this in reverse. When copying a frame into PawPrints, drag it to leave a space to write the title. Then drag the frame over the text. In PawPrints you can bring images to the front from the tools menu.

Skills To Learn | Combining images in a paint document

1 Select a colour to fill the page.
2 Click ▧ and click ▪.
3 Click on the page to fill it.
4 Select a different colour.
5 Click ✎, click ● and draw some shapes.
6 Click ✎, click ● or ▸, and draw some solid shapes.

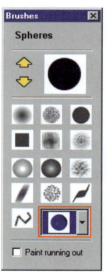

● and ▸ are in the picture section here.

7 Click ▫. Use each tool in turn to select and move part of the picture. Each tool can be used in a different way.

If you select and move parts of the picture you will leave a space.

8 Click ✎, and experiment with other brushes.
9 Click ▫. Use the selection tools to make abstract pictures.

You cannot resize the parts of this picture in Fresco.

Write about your picture.
1 Use ▫ or ○ to select a part of your picture.
2 Copy and paste it into PawPrints.
3 Select the picture and drag the green handles to resize it.
4 Write on the same page how you made your pattern.
5 Click 🖨 to print out your work.

Graphical modelling Unit 5A

Lesson Link — Art (F) (PP)

Design a frame.
1. Click ▢.
2. In the `Paper Size:` box, select **A4**.
3. In the `Orientation:` box, select **Portrait**.
4. In the `Paper Texture:` box, select **Rough weave**.
5. Click `View` and click `Zoom out` until you can see the whole page.
6. Click ✎, select 🍃, and draw a rectangle to frame the page.

Make a title page or poster.
1. Click , select , and copy and paste the page into PawPrints.
2. Click `View` and click `Zoom out` until you can see the whole page.
3. Type a title and select it.
4. In the text size box `12` ▾, click ▾ and select **48**.
5. To make the text fit inside the leaf border, click on it and drag the green handles.

Lesson Link — Technology (F) (PP)

Garden design
1. Click , select and draw a thin rectangle.
2. Click ✎ and select 🍃.
3. Click ⬇ to make the spray small.
4. Spray leaves over the rectangle.
5. Click ✎ and click ●.
6. Add colour to make a flowerbed.
7. Copy to PawPrints.
8. Copy and paste the picture to give you more flowerbeds.
9. Make them into a garden plan.

Off Screen

- Cut pictures and patterns from magazines and combine them to make a collage picture.
- Draw pictures of flowerbeds, trees, a lawn and pool, seen from above.
- Cut out and rearrange them to make a garden plan.
- Add paths and other details.
- Make a key to explain the symbols.

11

Unit 5A Graphical modelling

Changing shapes

Graphic elements can be moved, rotated, and resized

PawPrints

Shape boxes cannot be linked. Copies of shapes made initially, at the back, will always appear at the front, unless sent to the back.

Skills To Learn | Combining shapes

Put shapes in front and behind.

1 Click , select and draw a star.
2 Set the `Fill Colour` and `Line Colour` to blue.
3 Click , select and draw a circle.
4 Set the `Fill Colour` and `Line Colour` to yellow.
5 Drag the circle onto the star.

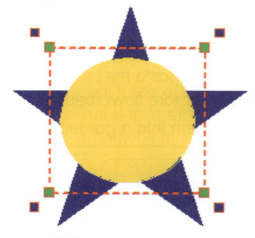

6 Click .
7 Click and and practise sending the yellow circle to the front or the back.

Group shapes.

1 Click to bring the circle to the front.
2 Click `Edit` and click `Select all`.
3 Click and select to join the shapes together.
4 Select the shape and drag the green arrows to resize it.
5 Select the shape and drag the blue arrows to rotate it.
6 Experiment with changing the line and fill colours.
7 Make the lines thick and dotted.

Click here to add a shadow to your picture.

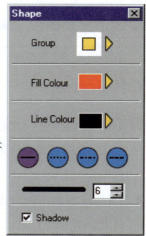

Graphical modelling **Unit 5A**

Lesson Link — Science

Circuit diagrams

1 Click [icon], select [□] and draw a square.
2 Set the `Fill Colour` to white.
3 Set the `Line Colour` to black.
4 Make it into a rectangle.
5 Click [icon], select [○] and draw a small circle.
6 Set the `Fill Colour` to white.
7 Set the `Line Colour` to black.
8 Select the circle and drag it onto the edge of the rectangle.
9 Click , select and draw a cross in the circle.

Put a gap in a circuit by adding a white rectangle with white edges.

10 Use lines for cells and switches.
11 Use circles for bulbs and bells.
12 Make a key to show what each symbol represents.

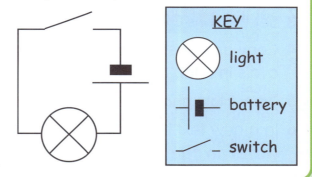

Lesson Link — Art PP F

1 Look at works of art by Kandinski, Mondrian and Klee.
2 Use lines and shapes to make similar pictures.

Experiment to see if the paintings are best done in Fresco or in PawPrints.

Off Screen

▸ Draw around shapes to make circuit diagrams. Label them and explain what is happening in each circuit.

▸ Use coloured paper shapes and felt tip pens to make collage pictures in abstract styles.

Unit 5A Graphical modelling

Making charts

 PawPrints

Geometric tools can create objects which can be manipulated

It can be useful to zoom out before you start to see a whole page. This will help with the placing of shapes and lines. You can zoom in again to check the details. If shapes obscure text pupils should be shown how to bring them forward using the tools menu.

Skills To Learn | **Combining shapes and text to make charts**

1 Click 🔲, select ⚪ and draw an oval.

2 Set the `Fill Colour` to white.

3 Set the `Line Colour` to black.

4 Copy and paste to make four ovals in total.

5 Type: Flow chart for making tea.

6 In a new text box type: Is there water in the kettle?

7 Drag one of the ovals to frame the question.

8 Type: Yes below the question and No to the right of the question.

Click ⊖, select ⊖ and draw lines like this.

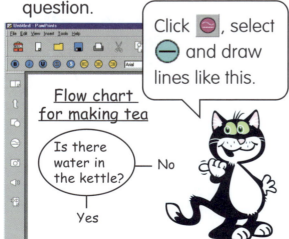

9 Type: Fill the kettle next to the word No. Add a frame to the text.

10 Type: Turn on the kettle under the word Yes.

11 Add an arrow from Fill the kettle to Turn on the kettle.

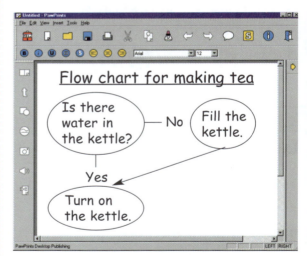

Continue to add questions (framed with ovals), and instructions (in text frames).

12 Add arrows to complete instructions to make a cup of tea.

Graphical modelling Unit 5A

Lesson Link | Technology

A 'get ready for painting' flowchart.

1 Use these questions:
 - Is your space clear?
 - Is the table covered with paper?
 - Have you put out paints, brushes and a water pot?
 - Have you got some paper?

2 Add your own instruction boxes to deal with 'No' answers.

Add arrows to make the flowchart clear.

Lesson Link | Maths

Make a Venn diagram.

1 Click [icon], select [icon] and draw two pale-coloured circles.
2 Type **More than half** in one circle and **Less than half** in the other circle.
3 Type **-**, and select it.
4 In the text size box [12], click ▼ and select **36**.
5 Copy and paste it eight times.
6 Make eight fractions, e.g. $\frac{1}{8}$, $\frac{2}{5}$, $\frac{4}{5}$, $\frac{7}{8}$, $\frac{1}{16}$, $\frac{4}{6}$, $\frac{5}{7}$, $\frac{1}{10}$.

Click [icon], and let your friends try after you've had a go.

7 Drag each fraction to the correct circle.
8 Ask an adult to check your work.

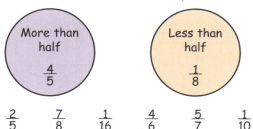

Off Screen

Bedtime flowchart

▸ Make a flowchart showing how you would avoid going to bed on time.
▸ Cut ovals for questions.
▸ Cut rectangles for instructions.
▸ Start with the question – **Have I got my drink ready?**

Unit 5A Graphical modelling

Exploring alternatives

A graphical model can be used to explore alternatives and ID patterns and relationships

Lesson Link

Pupils may need help to see that a plan view of an object is one which is seen from above.

Skills To Learn | Creating objects

1 Make plan views of the furniture in your class using the shape tools and line tools.

   To put shapes at the back or front click and use or .

2 Make a table like this:

3 Make a chair like this:

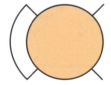

4 Make a bookshelf like this:

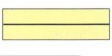

Remember to use colour.

5 Make a teacher's desk with drawers like this:

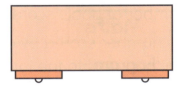

6 Add a key to remind you what each shape represents.

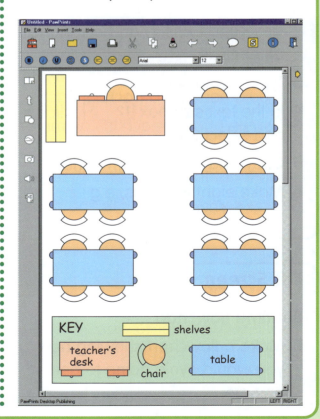

16

Graphical modelling Unit 5A

Lesson Link | Technology

Be your own architect!

1. Use the shapes you have made to plan your ideal classroom.
2. You could redesign the room you are in now.
3. Try joining the desks together.

Would it be easier to work if the desks were arranged another way?

Lesson Link | Maths   F   PP

Tessellating shapes.

1. In Fresco click , click and click ⬇ to make the pen small.
2. Click 🖼 and select ⬡.

Select **5** here to draw a pentagon.

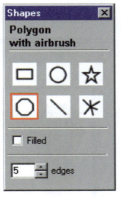

3. Copy and paste six copies of the shape into PawPrints.

4. Can you rotate and drag them to tessellate without any gaps?

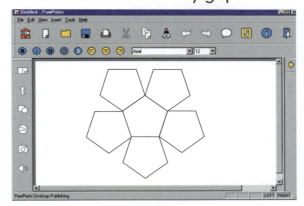

5. Try this with other shapes. Find out:
   - Which shapes tessellate with regular gaps.
   - Which shapes do not tessellate.

Off Screen

- Draw your classroom to a scale of 1 cm : 25 cm.
- Draw the furniture in the classroom to the same scale.
- Cut out the shapes to represent the furniture.
- Rearrange the shapes to find the best way to organise the room.

17

Unit 5A Graphical modelling

Designer school

Fresco

An object based graphics package can be used to explore a graphical model

You can hold **Ctrl** and tap − or + to zoom in and out quickly. Change to landscape view in the picture dialogue box

Skills To Learn | Exploring new layouts

School plan

1. In Fresco, click [icon].
2. In the Paper Size: box, select **A4**.
3. In the Orientation: box, select **Landscape**.
4. Click View and click Zoom out until you can see the whole page.
5. Look at a map of your school. Use it to help you paint a plan of the school.
6. Copy and paste your plan into PawPrints.

Click [icon] and click here to make the page landscape.

7. Click View and click Zoom out until you can see the whole page.
8. Drag the plan to fit the page.

Add to the plan.

1. Go back to Fresco and design plan views of trees, flower beds and play areas.
2. Copy each one to your PawPrints plan.
3. Move each feature into position and resize to fit.

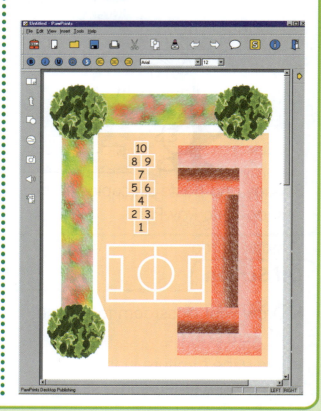

Graphical modelling Unit 5A

Lesson Link PE F PP

Create your own PE layouts.

1. In Fresco, draw graphics of the equipment you use in PE lessons.
2. Copy and paste them into PawPrints.
3. Design a layout for circuit training, to give a balance of exercises for strength, stamina and suppleness.
4. Design a layout for outdoors to give you a circuit of skills activities.

Lesson Link Technology F PP

Re-design your garden.

1. Click and in the Orientation: box, select **Portrait**.
2. Click View and click Zoom out until you can see the whole page.
3. Click , select O, and draw three overlapping green circles.
4. Click and fill the circles.
5. Choose a pale brown, click and fill the rest of the page.
6. Click , select , click and spray carefully over the green circles to make a lawn.
7. Click , select , and paint a stone border.
8. Paste it into PawPrints and add plants, trees, a path and a pond.

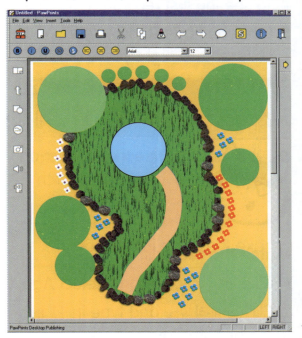

Off Screen

- Design a wildlife area for your school, e.g. a pond, pile of rotting logs, berry bushes, dry-stone wall.
- Ask your teacher if it would be possible to add any of these features to your school.

Unit 5B Analysing data and asking questions using complex searches

Data search

Information Workshop 2000

A database can be searched using =< & =>

Pupils should be aware that there are many types of database which are not electronic such as the school register, yellow pages and encyclopaedias.

Skills To Learn | Searching a database

1. Open Information Workshop and select ⊙ Load an existing file.
2. Click Next.
3. Select **Survey** and click OK.
4. To see the first record click OK.
5. Can you find out how many children are eight years old?

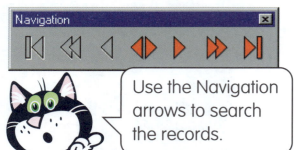

Use the Navigation arrows to search the records.

Match the records.

1. Click 👀, click ▼ and select **Age**.
2. Click equal to... and type in **11** in the bottom box.
3. Click OK and click Start search.

This = search finds all the children who are eleven years old.

Search favourite foods field.

1. Click 👀 and click Clear all.
2. To see a list of the records click 🗔.
3. Is your favourite food on the list?
4. Click 👀, click ▼ and select **Food**.
5. Click the same as... and select your favourite food in the bottom box.
6. To find others who like the same food as you click OK and click Start search.

Less than search (<).

1. Click 👀 and click Clear all.
2. Click 👀, click ▼ and click **Height**.
3. Click less than... and type **120** in the bottom box.
4. Click OK and click Start search.

This will find children less than 120cm tall. How many of these are there?

5. Now find how many children are more than (>) 140 cm tall.

Analysing data and asking questions using complex searches Unit 5B

Lesson Link | Science

1 Find out some facts about the solar system.

> Look at a children's encyclopedia on a CD ROM

2 Search for all the planets which have moons.

3 Search for planets with more than ten moons.

4 Search for planets which are less than 300 million miles from the sun.

Lesson Link | Geography

1 Open Information Workshop and select ⊙ Create a new file .
2 Click Next .
3 Select ⊙ Use the simple file setup .
4 Click Next .
5 Select ⊙ Choose a topic .
6 Click Next .
7 Select ⊙ Countries . Click Next .
8 Click in these boxes: Name, Area and Population, then
9 Click Finish .

Add information.

1 Find out information on two different countries.
2 Add the data by clicking on ✎.
3 Search the database to find:
- Countries with a population greater or smaller than the UK (population 56 million)
- Countries with an area greater or smaller than the UK
- Countries which start with the letter E.

Off Screen

▸ Collect more data for your countries database. Find out the maximum and minimum temperatures for the countries of your choice.

▸ Find out the average rainfall for these countries.

▸ Enter the data into the database and plan some more searches using < and > and =.

21

Unit 5B Analysing data and asking questions using complex searches

Search AND search

Information Workshop 2000

Searches can be carried out using more than one criterion (And searches)

It should not take long to set up a number database if each child in the class chooses 3 or 4 numbers and adds the data for those numbers to the database. This resource can be extended annually by each class using the database.

Skills To Learn | Using AND searches

Search to find two fields at once, e.g. children with red hair AND green eyes.

1. Open Information Workshop and Click `Load an existing file`.
2. Click `Next`.
3. Select **Survey** and click `OK`.
4. Click `OK` to see the first record.
5. Click `👀`, click `▼` and select **Hair Colour**.
6. Click `the same as...` and select **red** in the bottom box.
7. Click `OK` and click `and`.
8. Click `▼` and select **Eye Colour**.
9. Click `the same as...` and select **green** in the bottom box.
10. Click `OK` and click `Start search`.

Do any of the children have your eye and hair colour?

More AND searches

1. Find how many children have birthdays in August and like fish.
2. Find how many children are over 150 cm and weigh less than 35 kg.
3. Search three categories to find if there are more blue-eyed blonde girls or blue-eyed blonde boys.

Suspect search

1. Find the name of these two suspects using Survey database.
   - Someone with long arms reached in though a window and stole a purse. An ice cream wrapper was found below the window. A boy was seen running away.
   - The guard dog was tied up with a curry-stained tie. The thief must have been at least ten years old to have been allowed into the youth club.

Analysing data and asking questions using complex searches — Unit 5B

Lesson Link — Maths

1. Open Information Workshop and select **Create a new file**.
2. Select **Use the simple file setup**.
3. Select **Make your own file**.
4. Click **Next**.
5. Give your datafile a name.
6. Write a description of your file.
7. In the **Number of fields:** box, select **6**.
8. Give your datafile a name.
9. Click **Next**.
10. Enter these fields.
    - number name, e.g. 1,2,3,4,5...
    - is it odd/even?
    - is it a square number?
    - is it a triangular number?
    - is it a multiple of 3?
    - is it a multiple of 5?
11. Click ✏ and add data on the numbers 1 to 30.
12. Click 💾 and name your file **Number Database**.
13. Search the database to see which numbers are:
    - multiples of 3 AND 5
    - triangular AND multiples of 3
    - square AND triangular.

Lesson Link — History

1. Search a CD-ROM or the internet to find:
   - inventions by English people during the Second World War
   - pop groups which are female and have sold over 1 million albums
   - a list of pharaohs of Egypt.

Off Screen

- Collect data on numbers to add to the numbers database.
- Find answers to the history searches without using a database.

What are the advantages or disadvantages of searching for data in other ways?

Unit 5B Analysing data and asking questions using complex searches

OR searches

Information Workshop 2000

Search using OR, sift information and modify a search strategy

Pupils may think an AND search will produce more results than a simple OR search. Try this quick example: How many of you are boys? How many of you are boys AND have birthdays in June. How many of you are boys OR have birthdays in June.

Skills To Learn | Making an OR search

Children with blue OR green eyes.

Search to find one field OR another, e.g. children with blue or green eyes.

1. Open Information Workshop and click ⦿ Load an existing file .
2. Click Next .
3. Select **Survey** and click OK .
4. To see the first record click OK .
5. Click 👀 , click ▼ and select **Eye colour**.
6. Click the same as... and select **blue** in the bottom box.
7. Click OK and click or .
8. Select **green** in the bottom box.
9. Click OK and click Start search .

Children with long arms OR who are tall.

1. Click 👀 and click Clear all .
2. Click 👀 , click ▼ and click **Height**.
3. Click greater than... and type **150** in the bottom box.
4. Click OK and click or .
5. Click ▼ and select **Reach**.
6. Click greater than... and type **140** in the bottom box.
7. Click OK and click Start search .

More searches

1. Try these searches. Find children:
   - with birthdays in the summer holidays (July or August)
   - who are less than 1.25 m tall or who weigh less than 20 Kg
   - who like chicken or beefburgers.

Remember to click Clear all between your searches or you may limit the number of records you are searching.

Analysing data and asking questions using complex searches Unit 5B

Lesson Link — Maths

1. Open Information Workshop and click ⦿ Load an existing file.
2. Click Next.
3. Select **Number Database** (p23) and click OK.
4. Click OK to see the first record.
5. Use OR searches in your number database to find:
   - numbers which are multiples of 3 OR 5
   - numbers which are triangular OR square
   - numbers which are > 25 OR triangular OR multiples of 5.
6. Invent your own searches.
   - Show your answers to a friend.
   - Get them to guess the search you made to get them.

Here's a test for you! What search did I do to find the numbers 17, 19, 21, 23, 25 and 27?

Lesson Link — Science

1. Use a CD-ROM to find out about birds. Find out which birds:
   - visit Britain in winter OR summer
   - eat fish OR have webbed feet
   - eat seeds OR fruit.

I prefer cats! Find which cats live in Africa, OR which ones are domestic.

Off Screen

- List different contexts where an OR search might be useful, e.g.
  - I want to grow plants which flower in winter Or those which have coloured bark in winter.
  - I want a recipe which is either a fish dish OR a vegetarian recipe.
  - I want to know which footballers have scored more than 100 goals OR who have played for England.

Unit 5B Analysing data and asking questions using complex searches

Complex searches

To use complex searches to locate information

If using the Oxford Children's encyclopaedia remember to check the appropriate boxes on the right of the Find box. Skills to learn:- To use a combination of AND and OR searches.

Skills To Learn — To use a combination of AND and OR searches

Simple search

1 Open the encyclopaedia.
2 Click .
3 Type **nests** in the **Find...** Box.

> This will show all the pages which include the word nests.

4 Click **Find**.

> Note the number of entries you find.

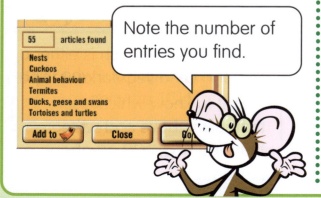

AND search

1 Click .
2 Type **nests** in the **Find...** box.
3 Type **birds** in the **and** box.
4 Click **Find**.

> This shows all the pages which include the word nests AND birds – there are fewer of these.

NOT search

1 Click .
2 Type **nests** in the **Find...** box.

> Click here and select **not**.

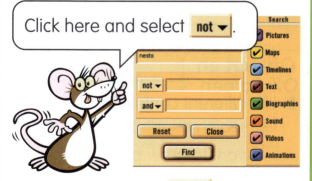

3 Type **birds** in the **not** box.
4 Click **Find**.

Analysing data and asking questions using complex searches Unit 5B

Lesson Link | Science

1. Click 🐘 and search for entries about flowering plants OR trees.

2. Search for entries about flowering plants NOT trees. This gives fewer entries.

3. Search for entries about trees NOT flowering plants. This gives more entries.

4. Search for entries about flowering plants AND trees. This gives fewer entries.

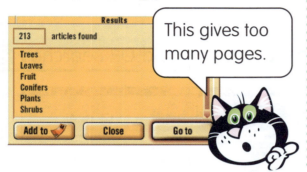

This gives too many pages.

Lesson Link | History

1. Search for inventions.
2. Search between 1000 BC and 2000 BC.
3. Search between 1000 AD and 2000 AD.
4. Search for Prime Ministers between two pairs of dates.

Enter the dates here.

You can limit the search by selecting `and` Britain or `not` Britain.

Off Screen

- Try hands-up surveys of your friends to see if more of them like football OR dancing.
- Do the same to find out who likes football AND dancing.
- Do the same to find out who likes football but NOT dancing.
- Graph your results and write about what they tell you about your class.

Unit 5C Evaluating information, checking accuracy and questioning plausibility

Problems with data

 Information Workshop 2000

To check for accuracy and anomalies using graphical representations

When the pupils are changing the survey database make sure you keep an untouched version of the database. Ensure they 'Save as' when saving their altered version. The program will prompt them to do this.

Skills To Learn | Spotting mistakes

1. Look at these charts. Each has a mistake. Can you spot what it is?
2. Draw the graphs again and put in more sensible data.

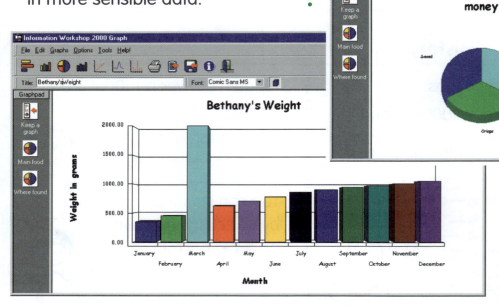

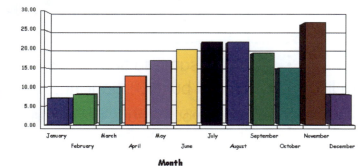

Bethany is my owner's little baby. She is very cute!

Evaluating information, checking accuracy and questioning plausibility — Unit 5C

Lesson Link — Maths

1. Open Information Workshop and click `Load an existing file`.
2. Click `Next`.
3. Select **Survey** and click `OK`.
4. Which of the following questions CANNOT be answered by looking at the database?
   - Are boys taller than girls?
   - Were the heaviest five children in the Black Cat survey also the five tallest children?
   - Do children with summer birthdays prefer chicken or beefburgers?
   - Which children like chocolate pudding best?
   - Is Matthew over or under 1.5 m?
   - Were more boys born in the summer or in the winter?

Explain your ideas to a friend.

Lesson Link — Science

Use line graphs to help spot errors.

1. Open the **Survey** file.
2. Click `Edit`, and select `Add record`.
3. Add a new record containing a deliberate error.
4. Challenge your friends to find the error by making a line graph.

Draw a line graph which correlates age and height.

5. Ask one of your friends to add another record with a deliberate mistake, and see if you can find it.

Off Screen

- Make three deliberate errors in a short piece of writing. Ask a friend to spot them.
- Check their work for mistakes.
- List some facts about an animal. Put in two pieces of data which are untrue. Ask a friend to find your mistakes.

Unit 5C Evaluating information, checking accuracy and questioning plausibility

Checking data

Information Workshop 2000

To identify and correct implausible and inaccurate data

The pupils could collect data about three famous people as part of a homework task.

Skills To Learn | Check for implausible or inaccurate data

Data errors

1 Data may include many different types of mistake:
 - spelling mistakes, e.g. Am**m**erica
 - unlikely data, e.g. **10 m** for the size of a mouse
 - a written entry in a number field, e.g. **ten** not **10**
 - a number entry in a text field, e.g. **4** not **four**
 - the word **male** or **boy** when the field asks for **m**
 - inaccurate data, e.g. York train departs 14.10 arrives 13.30.

Famous people database

1 Open Information Workshop and select ⊙ Create a new file .
2 Select ⊙ Use the simple file setup .
3 Select ⊙ Make your own file .
4 Click Next .
5 Give your datafile a name.
6 Write a description of your file.

7 In the Number of fields: box, select **7**.
8 Give your datafile a name.
9 Click Next .
10 Enter these fields.
 - Name
 - Male/female
 - Nationality
 - Date of birth
 - Date of death
 - Age on death
 - Reason for fame
11 Click ✏ and add the data.
12 Each person in the class should add one famous person's data to the database, but include one deliberate mistake.
13 Take it in turns to spot the deliberate error in each record.

How many errors can you find which are not deliberate?

Evaluating information, checking accuracy and questioning plausibility Unit 5C

Lesson Link — History

1 Click `Edit` and click `Find...` to quickly search the database for information on a famous person.

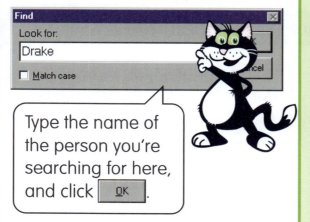

Type the name of the person you're searching for here, and click `OK`.

2 Use the computer to make a bar chart to show the age of people when they died. If some bars are unusually long or short they may show up big errors. They will not show up small errors.

3 Work with a friend to check each other's data.

Lesson Link — RE

World religions

1 Find some data about how many people follow each of the world's major religions.

2 Click  or to draw pie and bar charts to show your results.

3 Compare your charts with others in a children's encyclopedia on a CD-ROM, in an atlas or on the internet.

4 Do all the charts look the same?

5 Is all the data the same?

List all the reasons you can think of to explain the differences in the data and the charts.

Off Screen

- It is often easier to spot someone else's mistakes than your own.
- Start a writing partnership with a friend. Help each other by checking the writing that you do in each subject.
- Check for spelling, grammar and punctuation errors.
- Do you understand what they have written?
- Help each other to improve your writing.

Unit 5D Introduction to spreadsheets

Starting spreadsheets

 NumberBox 2

 Labels and numbers can be entered into a spreadsheet to calculate costs

Demonstrate the SUM command to the pupils.

Skills To Learn | Entering numbers into a spreadsheet

1 Click Start a new blank spreadsheet .
2 Click OK .

Spreadsheets are made up of cells. Each cell has an address. The address of this cell is C3.

This is a row.

This is a column.

Patterns

1 Put an X in each of these cells:
   A1 B2 C3 D4 E5 A5 B4 D2 E1
2 What pattern does this make?

Spreadsheets can add up.

1 Type these names in column A.
   Ali, Gareth, Elizabeth.
2 Type the number of letters each name has in column B.
3 Click in cell B6.
4 Click Formula and select Sum .

This adds the numbers in the column.

See the formula here.

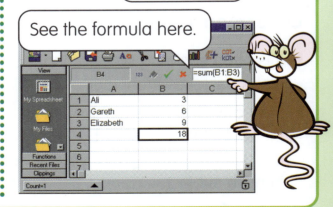

Introduction to spreadsheets Unit 5D

Lesson Link — Maths

Football scores

1. Click `File` and select `New`.
2. List the players in your favourite team in column A.
3. In column B show the goals they have scored.
4. Click `Formula` and select `Sum` to total the number of goals scored.
5. Change the number scored by a player. What happens to the total?

Pop score

1. List your favourite pop groups.
2. Put the number of group members in the next column.
3. Total the group members.
4. What happens when a group gains or looses a member?

My favourite group is the Boomtown Rats!

Lesson Link — Technology

1. Click `File` and select `New`.
2. List in column A the items you would need for a packed lunch.
3. List the price of each in column B.
4. Click `Formula` and select `Sum` to work out the total cost.
5. Alter some of the items and prices to see how the total cost changes.

Remember: Only put numbers in the column you want to add or the computer will not understand, e.g. 1.25 not £1.25.

Off Screen

- Use a calculator to work out the cost of different packed lunches.
- Which way do you like best... using a computer or a calculator?

Explain your reasons to a friend.

33

Unit 5D Introduction to spreadsheets

Maths machines

NumberBox 2

Formulae can be entered into a spreadsheet

Explain to the pupils that when they cut a section of text it stays in the computer's memory until another item is copied. This does not happen when they use the delete key.

Skills To Learn | Using simple formulae

An adding machine

1. Click `Start a new blank spreadsheet`.
2. Click `OK`.
3. Type a number in A1 and a number in C1.
4. In B1 type add.
5. In D1 type =.

Look, a formula box has appeared.

6. Click in A1.
7. Click `+` in the formula box.
8. Click in C1 and click ✓.
9. Cell D1 shows the sum of A1 and C1.

Change the numbers in A1 or C1. What happens in D1?

A take away machine

1. Double click in D1.
2. In the formula box delete + and click `−`.
3. Click ✓.
4. Change the word add to take in B1.
5. Change the numbers in A1 and A2. What happens in A3?

A multiplication machine

1. Double click in D1.
2. In the formula box delete − and click `×`.
3. Click ✓.
4. Change the word add to multiplied by in B1.

Multiplication puzzle

1. How far would everyone in your class stretch if laid end to end?

Hint: You will need to use an average height.

Introduction to spreadsheets   Unit 5D

Lesson Link — Maths

A division machine for sweets

1 Set out a spreadsheet like this.

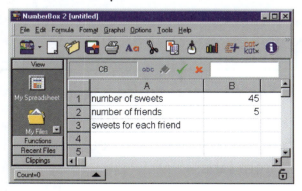

2 In B3 type =.
3 Click in B1.
4 Click / in the formula box.
5 Click in B2 and click ✓.
6 Cell B3 shows B1 divided by B2.

Try changing the number of sweets in B1, and the number of friends in B2.

Lesson Link — Science

My weight

1 Set out a spreadsheet like this:

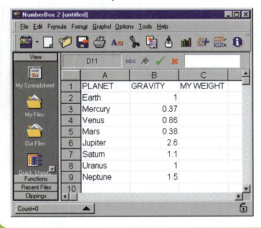

My weight on Mercury

1 In C3 type =.
2 Click in B3.
3 Click × in the formula box.
4 Click in C2 and click ✓.
5 Cell C3 shows C3 multiplied by C2.

My weight on other planets

1 Copy the formula and paste it into the other cells in Column C.

Off Screen

▸ Work out how much pocket money you have to spend every day, month, and year.

Use a calculator to help you.

35

Unit 5D Introduction to spreadsheets

Spreadsheet sums

NumberBox 2

Formulae can be used to calculate the total of a set of numbers in a range of cells

You can teach more able pupils to type formulae or let them use the icons. Click **Functions**, click **SUM** and specify the cells to be totalled and they will be totalled automatically.

Skills To Learn | Using formulae

Pocket money spreadsheet

1 Copy this spreadsheet of pocket money Tom has earned.

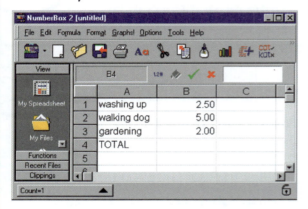

2 In B4 type =.

3 Type sum(B1:B3) and click ✓.

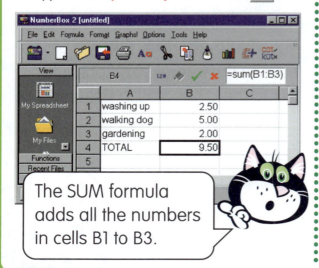

The SUM formula adds all the numbers in cells B1 to B3.

4 Design a spreadsheet to keep track of your pocket money.

5 Add the money you could earn from jobs.

Spending spreadsheet

1 What do you spend each week?

2 List each item you normally buy in column A.

3 Type TOTAL underneath them.

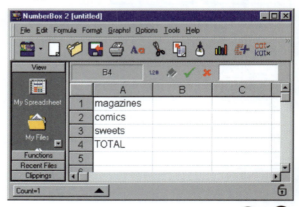

4 List the prices in column B.

Use the SUM formula to calculate the total.

5 Type the formula into the cell next to the Total.

Introduction to spreadsheets Unit 5D

Lesson Link — Maths

1 Copy this spreadsheet to work out the perimeter of the shapes.

Perimeter is the distance all the way round.

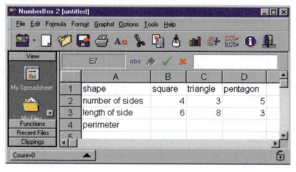

2 In B4 type =, and click in cell B2.

3 Click ✗ in the formula box.

4 Click in C3 and click ✓.

5 Cell B4 shows the perimeter of the square.

Copy and paste a formula.

1 Click in B4.

2 Select the formula and click 📋.

3 Click in the cell C4 and click 🖍.

4 Click in the cell D4 and click 🖍.

The program knows to change the formula when it is on a different row.

Lesson Link — History

1 In World War II people had 66 clothing coupons to last a year.

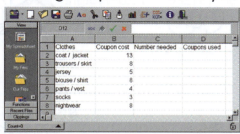

2 Type the number of each item you need in column C.

3 In D2 put the formula =C2*B2.

4 Copy and paste the formula into all the cells from D3 to D8.

5 In D9 type: =SUM(C2:C8) to see how many you have used in total.

Off Screen

▶ Use books to compare the cost of clothes in 1945 with those of today.

▶ Find out what camiknickers and combinations were.

Unit 5D Introduction to spreadsheets

Budgeting

NumberBox 2

Spreadsheets can be used to answer 'what if' questions

Spreadsheets allow pupils to change entries and see what happens to the totals.

Skills To Learn | Making choices using spreadsheet data

Loading a boat.

- Nina wants to rescue animals from an island that is going to flood.
- Her boat will sink with more than 4000 kg of animals.
- She must take at least one of each type.
- Use a spreadsheet to help her work out how many of each she could take.
- How many animals can she take in all?

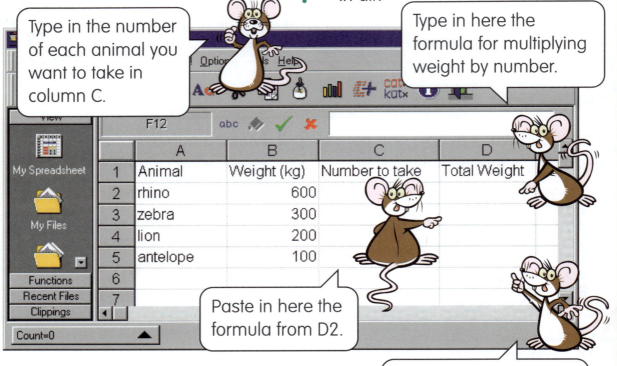

Type in the number of each animal you want to take in column C.

Type in here the formula for multiplying weight by number.

Paste in here the formula from D2.

Type a formula here to add up all the columns.

Introduction to spreadsheets Unit 5D

Lesson Link — Technology

Party spreadsheet

- Max only has £12 to spend on his party.
- He has six friends coming.
- Help him decide what to buy.

Put the total cost for each item in column D.

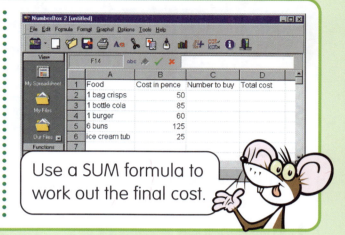

Use a SUM formula to work out the final cost.

Lesson Link — Science

Calculate averages.

The average formula evens out the high and low numbers.

1. Roll a car down a ramp three times.
2. Enter into a spreadsheet how far it goes each time.

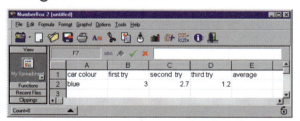

3. Click in cell E2.
4. Click **Formula** and select **Average**.

This is the average formula for the cells B2 to D2.

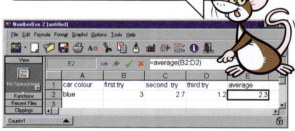

5. Now try with different cars.
6. Now try with a steeper ramp.

Off Screen

- Roll a car down a ramp three times and record the distances.
- Total the distances and divide by three to find the average.

Unit 5E Controlling devices

Sequences

A control box and software can be used to control one or more output devices

You will need a mains timer switch plus the leaflet. Remind pupils of mains dangers and do not allow them to plug into the mains without direct supervision.

Skills To Learn — Control the way simple devices switch on and off

Switches

- Many devices are turned on and off using switches.
- These include:
  - room lights
  - television
  - radio

- List some other devices which are controlled by simple switches.

Timer switches

- Many devices are on timer switches and follow a sequence.
- These include:
  - traffic lights
  - lamps on timer switches
  - central heating
- List some other devices which follow a sequence.

Traffic lights

1. Watch the sequence of traffic lights at a pelican crossing.
2. How do the pedestrian lights fit into the traffic light sequence?
3. Complete the pedestrian light sequence.

Phase	Traffic light	Pedestrian light
1	red	green
2	flashing amber	
3	green	
4	amber	
5	red	
6	flashing amber	
7	green	

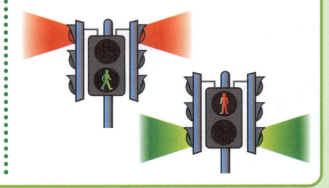

Controlling devices Unit 5E

Lesson Link | Technology

Timer switches

Timer switches are used to turn mains devices on and off.

1. Read the instructions on the pack.
2. Set the time correctly.

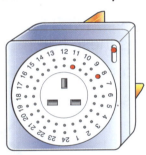

3. Set the device to turn:
   - **on** in about 30 minutes time
   - **off** 10 minutes before the next break
   - **on** 10 minutes after you come back in the room
   - **off** 10 minutes before home time.
4. Ask your teacher to plug it into the wall and plug in the device.

These timer switches can turn lamps and washing machines on and off.

Lesson Link | Science

Switches

1. Make a simple switch like this to control all kinds of devices.

Press the foil together to make the light come on.

2. Devise a switch like this that will work when someone treads on it.

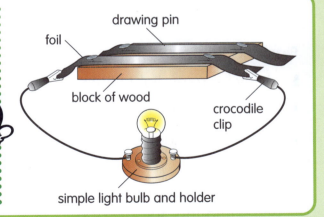

Off Screen

▶ Devise a switch which works when it is tilted.

▶ Hint: a foil-covered ball might be very useful.

41

Unit 5E Controlling devices

Control box

Output devices can be controlled by building a sequence of events to solve a problem

You will need to use a control box, which is plugged into a computer. Check the voltage of the bulbs required – 6 volts are usual.

Skills To Learn — Use a computer to switch a device on and off

The equipment

- A control box has output sockets to plug your devices into. It also has sockets for inputs but we will not be using these in this module.
- Control software runs the control box.

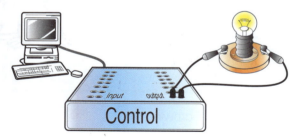

Flashing lights

- Many warning lights flash.
- Make your own flashing light.
- Make a simple circuit without a battery.
- Break the circuit and plug the wires into the pair of sockets marked 1.

> You are using the output sockets like a switch.

Software

- Consult the instruction booklet for your control equipment to check it recognises these commands.
- Start the control software.
- Type in a sequence of instructions.
  REPEAT
  SWITCH ON 1
  WAIT 10
  SWITCH OFF 1
  WAIT 10
  AGAIN

> The repeat/again instructions tell the computer to keep doing it.

Procedure

- Check the sequence works.
- Turn it into a named procedure.
  BUILD flash
  REPEAT
  SWITCH ON 1
  WAIT 10
  SWITCH OFF 1
  WAIT 10
  AGAIN
  END

Controlling devices Unit 5E

Lesson Link | Technology

Traffic lights

1. Make a set of three lights.
2. Colour them red, amber and green.
3. Plug the red into pair 1.
4. Plug the amber into pair 2.
5. Plug the green into pair 3.
6. Build a procedure in this way:
   BUILD traffic
   REPEAT
   SWITCH ON 1
   WAIT 10
   SWITCH ON 2
   WAIT 5

SWITCH OFF 1
SWITCH OFF 2
SWITCH ON 3
WAIT 20
SWITCH OFF 3
SWITCH ON 2
WAIT 10
SWITCH OFF 2
AGAIN
END

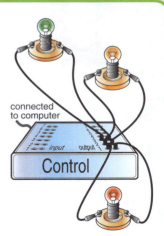

Change the timing and make it run more slowly or more quickly.

Lesson Link | Design and technology

1. Use PawPrints to design a clown.
2. Label the parts you need.

Build a clown face with bulbs for his eyes and a motor to whiz round a bow tie.

3. Add a buzzer to make a noise.
4. Plug each device into a pair of sockets.
5. Build a sequence to make his eyes flash, his tie turn and the buzzer sound.

Off Screen | Science

▶ Build a traffic lights set using simple circuits and switches.

▶ Ask your friends to describe the sequence of switch presses needed to make it work correctly.

43

Unit 5F Monitoring environmental conditions and changes

Monitoring changes

A computer can be used to monitor changes in environmental conditions

Every school will have its preferred methods and equipment for data logging, therefore the following pages are intended as overview and suggestion pages for how the equipment might be used.

Skills To Learn | Identify data which can be collected by sensors

1. List everyday situations in which environmental data is collected, e.g. weather forecasts, thermostats for central heating, monitoring traffic noise.

2. Discuss the problems involved in collecting data 24 hours a day in a variety of locations, e.g. domestic, urban, rural and maritime.

I used a sound sensor to detect the time when the birds start to sing in the morning.

3. Discuss ways in which such data can be displayed to make the results easier to see. Are written results, tables or graphs easier to understand?

Ask the caretaker about the movement sensors which turn on the burglar alarm and outside lights.

4. Explain which types of graph are most suitable for continuously changing data and which for spot check measurements.

5. List the places each sensor could collect data.
   - E.g. temperature sensor = warm water tap, cold water tap, hands, armpit, radiator.
   - Light sensor =
   - Sound sensor =

You could use a sound sensor in your school playground throughout the day.

Monitoring environmental conditions and changes Unit 5F

Lesson Link | Technology

Dough needs to be about 30°C to rise.

1. Where would it be best to put the dough to rise before baking? Use a temperature sensor to make spot checks of the temperature in different parts of the school.
2. Compare the readings you get with the readings from traditional thermometers. What differences do you find?

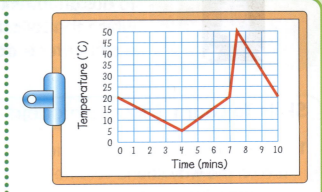

I took a temperature sensor round the school. Can you tell when I put it under the hot tap and in the fridge.

Lesson Link | Science

1. Freeze the end of a temperature sensor in an ice cube.
2. Plug the sensor into the computer and record the temperature as the ice melts and the water comes to room temperature.
3. Explain the shape of the resulting graph.

Off Screen

- Use forehead strip thermometers to measure your temperature before and after exercise.
- Do you get the results you expect?
- Explain the changes you record.
- See whose temperature changes the most.

Graph your results.

45

Unit 5F Monitoring environmental conditions and changes

Explaining data

To design investigations for which the collection of data by a computer is advantageous

It is interesting to create some artificial peaks in volume and light experiments so as to have interesting data to interpret. Perhaps a silent test situation could be followed by a noisier type of lesson. Lights switched on after dark for a while would give interesting peaks to explain in the resulting graph.

Skills To Learn | Analysing data

1. Use a computer data logger to record the way sound volume changes during a lesson.
2. Identify what was happening at each point in the graph.

How do computers make this an easy task?

3. Set a light sensor to monitor the classroom for 24 hours.
4. Identify the peaks and troughs on your graph.

Which were the lightest and darkest times?

5. Monitor the temperature changes in a classroom at different seasons of the year. This will give interesting data to compare and interpret.

6. Use two temperature sensors to compare the time it takes freezing water and very hot water to come to room temperature. List your ideas for the different rates.

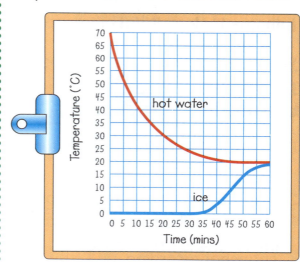

7. Compare the speed at which water cools in containers of different shapes, sizes and materials. Explain your findings.

46

Monitoring environmental conditions and changes Unit 5F

Lesson Link — Music

Comparing instrument volume.

1. Use sound sensors to compare the volumes of different types of instrument.
   - Do brass instruments sound louder than woodwind or string instruments?
   - Does it make a difference how each is played?
2. Ask the same person to put the same amount of energy into playing different percussion instruments.

Try to explain the differences in volume you record.

Lesson Link — Science

Which sunglasses give the most protection?

1. As part of a health education project, see which types of sunglasses give the most protection to your eyes.
2. Hold each pair of glasses over the light sensor and make a snapshot recording.
3. Which types of coloured lens keep out the most light?
4. Is this the only factor to consider when buying sunglasses?
5. Write a health education leaflet to explain your ideas.

Off Screen

- Use the volume control on a tape-recorder to see who has the most sensitive hearing in the class.
- You will need to record a continuous sound such as a buzzer to make this a fair test.

47

Glossary

AND search	Looking for information in a database using the word AND between questions.	**handles**	The points which can be dragged to change the shape of a graphic.
cell address	The co-ordinate of a cell which has a letter and number.	**OR search**	Looking for information in a database using the word OR between questions.
column	The vertical columns in a spreadsheet table.	**orientation**	The way a page is seen. Horizontal layout is landscape. Vertical layout is portrait.
complex search	Looking for information in a database using more than one question at a time.	**resize**	To change size of a graphic by dragging its handles.
control box	A device which turns switches on and off using the computer.	**resize**	To change size. Objects can be made larger or smaller on screen.
data	Information.	**right click**	To press the right mouse button this usually puts a menu on screen.
datalogging	Recording information onto the computer using sensors.	**rotate**	To turn a shape or word.
device	A machine which does a job	**row**	A horizontal line of boxes in a spreadsheet.
document	A single page or a series of pages.	**select**	Graphics are selected by throwing a selection rectangle or lasso around them.
draw	To make shapes and lines using draw tools.	**sensor**	A device which monitors changes such as temperature, light or sound.
fill	To flood a shape with colour or pattern.	**sequence**	A pattern of events or commands.
flowchart	A diagram which shows the order in which events occur.	**spreadsheet**	Rows and column of data stored in cells.
font	The style of text.	**zoom**	To magnify or shrink an image on the computer screen.
formula	A calculation.		
graphic	A picture.		
group	To make a several objects or parts of a drawing into one item.		